# VIRTUAL CURRENCIES AND IMPLICATIONS OF ANTI-MONEY LAUNDERING REGULATIONS

## VOLUME 2, ISSUE 2 OF BRILLOPEDIA

MEDISHETTY MANASWINI

# Contents


*Preface*                                                                                    *v*

*Author*                                                                                   *vii*

1. Abstract                                                                                    1

2. Introduction                                                                               3

3. Evolution Of Anti-money Laundering Regulation In India              6

4. Existing Situation                                                                       10

5. Risks Involved                                                                            13

6. Money Laundering Through Decentralised Virtual Currencies      15

7. Judicial Pronouncements                                                            17

8. Global Approach                                                                         20

9. Recommendations/suggestions                                                  22

10. Conclusion                                                                              23

# Preface

"Start writing, no matter what. The water does not flow until the faucet is turned on".

-Louis L'Amour

Hundreds of students and professors are contributing their work to Brillopedia, we are here to provide ample information about Law and Contemporary issues. Our aim is to provide a platform for today's generation to express their views and ideas on law and contemporary law.

# Author

# CHAPTER ONE

# ABSTRACT

Virtual currencies are something that is digitally traded and acts as a medium of exchange. Virtual currencies do not have any kind of legal status. It does not have any legal status in any jurisdiction. It is only based on the agreement between the users of the virtual currency. Virtual currency is different from the Real currency which shall be accepted legally and issued in any country. As in recent years, we can see an increase in decentralized virtual currencies in which the concept of cryptocurrencies has increased drastically. To have transactions generally, depends on the KYC (Know your customer) and CIP (Customer Identification Process). Certain standards are fixed global and it is expected the countries to follow those rules. By now most the countries included in their domestic law and follow them. India has proven its interest in virtual currencies, because as of July 2021 it has been said that nearly 15 million investors are holding more than the US $ 13 million worth of virtual currencies. The main objective of this paper is about virtual currencies and what are the risks involved when it comes to Money Laundering. The Researcher also tried to focus on the regulations that are implemented by the SEBI and RBI regarding FATF. The paper also talked about convertible currency & non-convertible virtual currency and centralized and non-centralized virtual currencies. After reading this paper one can easily understand the virtual currencies and how they increased the money laundering and regulations that are introduced to combat the same. The object of the paper is to highlight the developments legally. Some judgments have changed the course of this issue and enlarged the meaning of some laws and rights. The research on this topic is done with the help of the Doctrinal Research method which includes taking relevant information from various reference books, online law portals, law journals, and the bare act. The assistance from teachers and seniors was availed at different junctures. The author has taken the help of newspaper articles, comments of various jurists, online legal databases, and other internet websites. The author's work is entirely based on analysis and research and the conclusions made therein.

In this paper, the researcher tried to find out the Anti-money laundering regulations regarding virtual currencies. When a researcher has read articles the researcher got to know about different kinds of virtual currencies and how they can be reliable. Money laundering has increased at the global level where recommendations are also given by the enforcement agencies but still, we can see the activities are going on. In this paper, research has been done regarding money laundering and how it can be decreased or combated.

# CHAPTER TWO

# INTRODUCTION

Virtual currency is the digital representation of value that does not have any legal status in any state, and it has mainly 3 functions are medium of exchange, a unit of account, and a store of value. These functions can only be filled by an agreement between the virtual currency users. Virtual currency is different from real money or paper money because it has legal status in a country and is accepted as a medium of exchange. E-money is electronically transferred the real money or fiat currency which has already legal status. Digital currency is always used interchangeably for e-money or virtual currency. Virtual currencies can be either convertible or nonconvertible and the administration can be centralized or decentralized.

Conversion of virtual currency is only possible when some private participant's offers are accepted by others which are not guaranteed by the law. A convertible virtual currency has a value that is equal to real currency and it can be traded for the real currency like e-gold and it can also be exchanged for the real money or vice-versa. Whereas non-convertible virtual currency has no equivalent value to real currency and it is intended to be restricted to a virtual domain and these domains can be exchanged for real money. Non-convertible currency can be officially transferred within a restricted virtual environment. Unofficially nonconvertible virtual currency can be exchanged for flat currency or other virtual currency which can be into black marketing. A non-convertible characterization is not necessary to be static.

As non-convertible virtual currencies are issued by the central authority so these currencies are centralized whereas convertible virtual currencies can either be centralized or decentralized. Centralized virtual currencies have a single administrative authority that issues the currency and is controlled by a third party. The exchange value of the virtual currency can be either determined based on market supply and demand or by the fixed value given by the administrator. In the present day, most virtual currency transactions involve centralized virtual currencies.

Cryptocurrencies/decentralized virtual currencies are virtual currencies that do not influence central administrating authority. These cryptocurrencies are math-based and convertible and it is protected by cryptography which is distributed decentralized and secured in nature. The transfer of these currencies is dependent on the individuals and it has to be signed each time cryptographically and then transferred.

The integrity and balance of cryptocurrencies are secured by mutually distributed parties who protect the network for a share of newly generated currency or for a transactional fee. In the case of bitcoins, miners protect the balance and gain a fractional part of the newly generated currency.

In the case of decentralized virtual currencies especially bitcoins there are two narratives. They are;

1. Virtual currencies are considered to be the future of payment systems.

2. It provides a medium for unlawful acts and transfers.

In the year 2013 New Payment Products and Services [NPPS] gave guidance to understand the framework and address the anti-money laundering and counterfeiting the financial funding to terrorism which was a great risk associated with the wired transactions or online transactions. A short-term typologies project based on this 2013 NPPS has been initiated with the following objectives:

1. To develop a risk grid for virtual currencies

2. To foster a complete knowledge of parties who got involved in the convertible virtual currencies system and its mode of operation

3. Implementing risk-based AML in the sector by stimulating the discussions.

Money laundering is the process that is generally used to generate assets based on criminal activity. It is a process where money is used for doing illegal activities. In money laundering, the illegal money is converted into legitimate money. There are three steps in money laundering; they are placement, layering, and Integration. In 2013 there was a report submitted by the Financial Intelligence Unit, which has said there are reports from banks that clearly says that clients receive huge amount through bitcoins which is a kind of virtual currency. Bitcoin wallet and Bitcoin address are not associated with any identity or name. This secrecy makes to do illegal activities. Bitcoin allows acquiring the money in such a manner that no one can identify it. The trade on the darknet markets is only paid by the bitcoin and most of the goods that are offered on the dark web are illegal. The attractive part of the bitcoin is the payment can be made in a few seconds where the identity of the sender and receiver are not mentioned, so here the greater secrecy is enjoyed. Virtual assets are the new way through which the laundering is being done by the criminals. There are mainly three money laundering categories for the trade-in of virtual currencies. They are:

1.  The withdrawal of the cash repeatedly from the bank without any necessity and the cashless receipts of the sum of money.
2.  When virtual currencies are being purchased then the identity of the buyer and seller are not revealed and there are high chances of money laundering.
3.  The buyer or the seller uses a mixer during the sale of virtual currencies.

# CHAPTER THREE

# EVOLUTION OF ANTI-MONEY LAUNDERING REGULATION IN INDIA

The Financial Action Task Force (FATF) is an inter-governmental body introduced at the G7 summit in Paris in 1989. It set certain standards for combating Money laundering and terrorism financing. FATF gives recommendations to the countries that are part of it and they should implement them in their own countries. FATF works in collaboration with the other International stakeholders to protect the International Financial system which might be misused. In 2002 the countries started adopting Money laundering laws and all the mechanisms to monitor all the financial transactions. At the International level for the first time to combat Money Laundering, we have the United Nations Convention against Illicit Traffic in Narcotics Drugs and Psychotropic Substances of 1988. This convention was mainly about Money Laundering and Drug Trafficking. In the year 1988, thcre was a committee formed Banking Regulations and Supervisory Practices; it has introduced KYC (Know Your Customer) policy. Finally, in the year 2000, we got the United Nations Convention against Transnational organized crime where most of the provisions were related to the Money Laundering and the international cooperation during the financial investigations.

India is a member of the United Nations Convention against Illicit Traffic in Narcotics Drugs and Psychotropic Substances of 1988 and became part of FATF in the year 2010 the some amendments took place in the legislation and the circulars were issued by the RBI. India was ranked 78th in the year 2016 on Anti-Money Laundering Basel Index. Before Prevention Money

Laundering Act 2002, there are other acts were introduced.

The Conservation of Foreign Exchange and Prevention of Smuggling Activities Act, 1974[1], was passed to have foreign exchange within the country and prevent smuggling activities. If an individual is found to involvement in smuggling activities then the executive has the power to detain them. This Act was passed based on Preventive Detention. After smuggling takes place, in return the individual who does get a huge amount of money from a hidden source. This Act talked about the apprehension of the smuggling and detaining of those individuals, but it did not talk about the money that is sent in the form of virtual currencies. Because this Act was introduced in the year 1974 according to the conditions that were prevailing at that time.

The Benami Transaction (Prohibition Act), 1988[2], was passed to prohibit the Benami transactions because here the Benami most of the time is a factious person. Any transaction in which property is transferred from one person for a considerable period and provided by another person. Benami transactions happen whenever the fraud is committed for tax evasion purposes, Money Laundering, etc.

The Indian Penal Code talks about the various criminal offences and at the same time provide the punishment for the offences. The procedure for the punishment is provided under the Criminal Procedure Code. In the prevention of Money Laundering, it has been mentioned that the proceedings are initiated according to the procedure mentioned in the Criminal procedure Code.

The Narcotic Drugs and Psychotropic Act, 1985, have passed against the acts relating to drug trading and restraint on the flow of money into the illegal activities. Prevention of Money Laundering Act (PMLA) -2002 was introduced to prevent money laundering and combat terrorism financing. PMLA Act, RBI regulatory, and SEBI work together to prevent Money Laundering. Finance Act got amended in the year 2015 which says that if the person who does the illegal activities or frauds or money laundering absconded from India then whatever the land or assets there in India can be confiscated. Again in the year, 2018 Finance Act was amended because if a person absconded then it is not easy to bring the person back hence PMLA act also got amended. Enforcement of the PMLA Act was criticized because fewer convictions, investigations, and prosecutions were done. When the PMLA act was introduced in the year 2002 it did not involve the lawyers, gen dealers, property dealers, etc. Hence amendments needed to be enhanced.

RBI gave certain guidelines that have to be followed by the banks to prevent money laundering and combat terrorism financing instead of recommendations given by FATF. Some of the guidelines are;

i.   Manual reporting of the day-to-day transactions.
ii.  Manual reporting of the suspicious transactions.
iii. Consolidated reporting has to be done by the principal officer of the bank.
iv.  Electronic data structures have to be reported.

Financial institutions should pay attention to the new technology that favors the transactions to take place online. According to the FATF recommendations, the RBI updates the circulars. The main purpose of KYC is to understand the individual account and the transactions related to it. KYC norms have mainly 4 elements, they are,

i.   Customer Acceptance Policy
ii.  Customer Identification process
iii. Monitoring process
iv.  Risk Management

India become part of FATF in the year 2010, so accordingly RBI and SEBI updated the circulars and amendments that took place in legislation. FATF released revised recommendations in the year 2015 regarding convertible virtual currencies. The main target was the virtual currencies and the traditional banking system that is already prevailing. The recommendations did not cover the internal market transfers. In 2019 the FATF gave recommendations regarding virtual assets. It has included virtual asset providers and imposed monitoring obligations on them. As of now virtual asset providers are subject to the money travel rule. The new FATF gives guidance that captures entities involved in the transfer of virtual assets, the safekeeping of virtual assets, and the provision of financial services related to an issuer's offer or sale of a virtual asset within the definition of virtual assets provider.[3]

The FATF recommendation in the year 2019 has also defined clearly virtual assets and virtual currency it said that it is the value i.e. digitally represented and digitally traded which is used for payment or investment purposes.

[1] The Conservation of Foreign Exchange and Prevention of Smuggling Activities Act, 1974, no 52, Acts of Parliament, 1974 (India).

[2] The Benami Transaction (Prohibition) Act 1988, No 45, Acts of parliament, 1988 (India).

[3] JD Candidate, INTERNATIONAL ANTI-MONEY LAUNDERING REGULATION OF VIRTUAL CURRENCIES AND ASSETS, Vol 52:875., NYU JILP, 875, 881, 2020, https://www.nyujilp.org/wp-content/uploads/2020/10/NYI304.pdf.

# CHAPTER FOUR

# EXISTING SITUATION

This covid-19 has created the investors to go for an alternative for the investments by which Cryptocurrencies are in demand. Cryptocurrency is a decentralized virtual currency that is dependent on blockchain technology. As purchases are not able to be traced the individuals use the purchase for illegal trade like drugs, firearms, etc. In the year 2021, the Cryptocurrency market value has crossed the $1 trillion but unofficially in the market, it suggests that investments show the US $1.4 billion. Most millionaires would invest in the cryptocurrencies like bitcoin, Ethereum, etc. RBI in the year 2018 had passed a circular in which it mentioned that banks are prohibited from extending the financial services that involve Cryptocurrency. There was a committee Inter-Ministerial committee formed by the Ministry of Finance which gave a report and said that the action has to be taken about the virtual currencies and save the customers from the fraud taking place, to protect the financial institutions. This committee has submitted the draft bill on Banning of Cryptocurrency and Regulation of Official Digital Currency Bill 2019, which is said to ban Cryptocurrencies. The bill also said the individual whoever directly or indirectly mines, generates, holds, sells, deals in, transfers disposes of, or issues cryptocurrency shall be punished with up to 10 years of imprisonment.[1]

In **Internet and Mobile Assn. of India V RBI,** the Supreme Court quashed the RBI circular and held that if access to the Cryptocurrency is denied for the users then it is equal to the denial to carry the trade or profession mentioned in article 19(1) (g) of the Constitution. Hence, the Bill was introduced in the year 2021 to prohibit all the private cryptocurrencies that operated in India. This might be considered because RBI is directed to set up its digital currency.

In the present world with cryptocurrencies that are inclined to Anti Money Laundering or counter-terrorism financing or cyber hackings, no country in the world has acknowledged the cryptocurrency as legally valid. The Supreme Court in case Internet and Mobile Assn. case said that RBI can put in picture about the Cryptocurrency and its definition would fit in Foreign Exchange Management Act, 1999. The court also said that Cryptocurrency does not have any monetary value and it cannot be assorted under the Payment and Settlement Systems Act, 2007 as a prepaid instrument. After the judgment has passed the Ministry of Corporate affairs made it obligatory that the companies who are trading the cryptocurrencies have to provide the profit and loss that has occurred on the transactions.

In most cryptocurrencies, the payment from where it is received cannot be found. Cryptocurrencies like Zcash, verge, Monero, Dash and Horizen somewhere help to find the parties who are involved in the transaction. Bitcoin records show that the criminals have laundered the US $2.8 billion through virtual currency exchange. As there is no proper law enforcement and authority to regulate Cryptocurrency it became easy for the criminals to launder huge. In Cryptocurrency when the transaction takes place the source from where funds are coming will not be traced which is violating the provision of the PMLA Act. Hence the financial institutions, banking companies, and intermediaries have to maintain and keep records. These nontraceable transactions made the criminals do money laundering. So we can say that unless this anonymity is removed then only cryptocurrency transactions can be traced or freezing of the digital wallet can be done, but this has become difficult for the Directorate of Enforcement. Indian Income-tax law is not clear about the gains and earnings through cryptocurrencies.

Money launderers always find a new way to launder; now internet became the new way to avoid tracing the source. The technology the being increased day by day and it helps the criminals to do Money laundering like the proxy servers tool which becomes impossible to trace the money that is being transferred to the person, the source cannot be found. Anti Money Laundering policies have to be followed by the banks and financial institutions.

India is a member of the International Convention of the Suppression of Financing of Terrorism-1999, United Nations Convention against Corruption, United Nations Convention against Transnational Crime and Financial Action Task Force since 2010 by which we got PMLA in the year 2002. As we do not have any procedures for cryptocurrency exchanges, while exchanges take place they use the penny drop method. In which they deposit 1 rupee in exchange wallet by which we can verify the bank details are correct or not. Many exchanges use Anti Money Laundering software which aids them to acknowledge the addresses of the cryptocurrency that are boycotted. As blockchain is decentralized and exchange takes place on a peer-peer basis it makes criminals exchange cryptocurrency through many hands. At last, the enforcement agencies cannot trace the money that has been withdrawn.

[1] Jai Anant Dehadrait and Md Tasnimul Hassantt, Cryptocurrency in India: An Unregulated Safe Haven For Money Laundering?, SCC online.com Blog (Apr. 9, 2022, 1:35 PM), https://www.scconline.com/blog/post/2021/09/28/cryptocurrency-in-india/.

# CHAPTER FIVE

# RISKS INVOLVED

Convertible Virtual currencies are those currencies that can be exchanged for flat currency and can be exposed to Money laundering and terrorism financing. Decentralized virtual currencies are prone to risks because during transfers transmitter and receiver are not identified. Historical records of transactions are very important because it keeps the record and helps in monitoring the transactions at any time, eliminating the ability to monitor leads to drastic effect, because in bitcoin transactions we cannot see the history of transactions by which there are chances for the commission of money laundering. As of now in India, there is no Anti Money Laundering rule to monitor or identify such anonymous transactions about virtual currencies.

Virtual currencies can be used via the internet and through phones also for payments at cross borders. In addition, virtual currencies commonly rely on complex infrastructures that involve several entities, often spread across several countries, to transfer funds or execute payments. This segmentation of services means that responsibility for AML/CFT compliance and supervision/enforcement may be unclear.[1]

Criminals have laundered around about $2.8 billion along with crypto-asset exchanges. Transactions in cryptocurrency have their pros and cons for illegal use or legal use. Every crypto asset exchange has risks involved in it. Money laundering became possible due to the anonymity in the cryptocurrency exchanges. Cryptoasset markets are not regulated or protected at the global level.

The main risks that are involved are:

1. The crypto asset or cryptocurrency exchanges are mostly linked with illegal activities like money laundering, terrorism, drug trafficking, etc. Here from where the fund is transferred or received the identity cannot

be traced. Sometimes a single crypto wallet can be linked with multiple banks & credit cards, where a group of people uses one wallet and funds which are to be moved.

2. When cryptocurrency transactions take place we find sometimes suspicious. Suspicious transactions like transferring multiple times, high-occurrence of the transactions of huge amounts from multiple wallets into one account in a single time and these wallets do not match with the profiles of the customer.

3. At the global level if we see the regulations of Anti-Money Laundering and KYC has to be made about the cryptocurrencies or virtual currencies. The protective measures are not being implemented by which scope is being given to the criminal groups to do illegal activities. In high-risk jurisdictions, suspicious patterns can be seen because of a lack of regulations and protections.

4. Monitoring of the high-frequency transactions should be done and regulations have to be made.


[1] FATF, Virtual Currencies – key definitions and potential AML/CFT risks, fatf-gafi.org., 3, 9, (2014), https://www.fatf-gafi.org/media/fatf/documents/reports/Virtual-currency-key-definitions-and-potential-aml-cft-risks.pdf.

# CHAPTER SIX

# MONEY LAUNDERING THROUGH DECENTRALISED VIRTUAL CURRENCIES

Bitcoin is a decentralized virtual currency combination of cryptography and peer-to-peer architecture which makes it avoid having authority at the center. Bitcoin is a virtual currency that is created first and is in the use. Through Bitcoin wallet exchanges funds from the owner account exchanged to bitcoin or exchanges cash into the bitcoins. The Federal Bureau of Investigation considers that bitcoin payments may pave the way for Money laundering and other illegal activities. As in the bitcoin system because of its anonymity, we cannot find the person who is doing it.

The law enforcement agencies may locate IP addresses in association with the transfer of the bitcoin but most criminals are advanced by which it becomes difficult to trace the transactions. The techniques that are used by the criminals to not be traced are; for each payment create a new bitcoin and use it, find the IP address of the bitcoin through the anonymizer, merging the old bitcoins addresses to the new address for making of the new payments, they use third person for money laundering the wallet service, using the specialized third party wallet service to merge with the several addresses to one wallet. The criminals using these techniques establish the direct bank accounts physically in countries where financial regulations are low which makes the transactions untraceable. The dark wallet is a new product that makes the anonymizer the techniques to have friendly money laundering that is operated by the criminals at an advanced level.

Virtual currencies like bitcoin, linden, dollar, etc are used in money laundering and terrorism financing because of their anonymity. These virtual economies were created as a result of massively-multiplayer online games (MMOGs) that allow players to exchange fiat currency for the game's virtual currency, which can be used to purchase various features within the game.[1]

In bitcoins, there is no centralized authority by which it becomes feasible for criminals to commit illegal activities. Criminals first buy the visa prepaid cards then they use these cards to buy the MMOG virtual currencies by using different player accounts and then resell the virtual currencies to others. Then use MSB in the foreign country by which funds are transferred to a legitimate financial institution.

[1] Berkely A Pamplin, Virtual Currencies and the Implications for U.S. Anti-Money Laundering Regulations, UMI number: 1564625, Pro Quest LLC, 1, 16, (2014), https://www.proquest.com/openview/1f7e0456bee46d7c0cf4aec953590cbb/1?pq-origsite=gscholar&cbl=18750&diss=y.

# CHAPTER SEVEN

# JUDICIAL PRONOUNCEMENTS

Internet and Mobile Association of India V Reserve Bank of India

Here, the writ petition was filed by the Internet and Mobile Association regarding the circular that was issued by the RBI which lacks the jurisdiction to forbid the trade of virtual currency.

**FACTS**

RBI passed a circular in 2018 which forbids the banks and other entities from trading in virtual currencies. It also mentioned that banks are not allowed to give any kind of help or services to individuals or companies about virtual currencies. This circular was passed to stop illegal activities because virtual currencies are at risk of money laundering, terrorist financing, etc.

**CONTENTIONS**

The petitioner contended that the circular issued by the RBI was just a misunderstanding and virtual currency is not money or fiat currency it is a medium of exchange according to the definition given by the FATF. The definition that was given by the FATF is 'Virtual currency' as a digital representation of value that can be traded digitally and functioning as (1) a medium of exchange; and/or (2) a unit of account; and/or (3) a store of value, but not having a legal tender status.[1]

RBI contended that it has jurisdiction and the digital payment. RBI alleged to the contention given by the petitioner that virtual currency is not the note or kind of currency, for this, it said that digital currency or virtual currency is something which is used in trading and virtual currency is operating independently without the interference of the government.

**JUDGMENT**

The court held that some entities accept virtual currencies as a valid form for procuring goods and services. And we cannot miss the point that the traders of virtual currencies do such activities that are under the RBI only. So RBI has the power to forbid any such activities. The circular that was passed by the RBI initially talked about the individuals who are regulated under the Payment and Settlement Act system.

Supreme Court has agreed with the contentions of the petitioner and said that the circular issued by the RBI is not reasonable and illegal. After this decision, businesses can be allowed to trade in cryptocurrencies. The Court had dissolved the circular of RBI but it has not declared that the virtual currencies are legal or illegal and in India, we do not have any specific legislation regarding the virtual currencies.

There is a Bill named Banning of cryptocurrency and Regulation of Official Digital Currency bill, 2019 which has been drafted but was never presented in the parliament.

**Hitesh Bhatia v. Mr. Kumar Vivekananda**, Case No. 3207 of 2020, decided on 1st July 2021

<u>FACTS</u>

The complainant is in the sale and purchase of the bitcoins. The offender has purchased bitcoins from the complainant on different occasions. Given the complainant when the accused transferred funds to the plaintiff (complainant) he would in return transfer the bitcoins to the accused virtual wallet. Then on 5th July 2020, he got to know that his bank accounts were frozen because they all are illegal transactions. He also mentioned the sources of the money paid against the bitcoins; at the same time the offender has accepted that the payments were a scam. The plaintiff applied section 156(3) of CrPC. Further Court had sought an action report to be submitted by the police.

The complainant submitted the following things to the court:

The counsel of the complainant has submitted that the court had jurisdiction in this case because all the transactions took place in Moti Nagar New Delhi. Secondly, the complainant has the right to have legitimate trade and profession under article 19(1) (g) of the Constitution. The complainant used to have payment of bitcoins through recorded medium and proceeds of crime but it was never seen in his intention and which was done due to lack of due diligence. Thirdly Cryptocurrency is not real money so it does not fall under the scope of RBI Regulations. Banning of Cryptocurrency and Regulation of Official Digital Currency Bill, 2019 has not been passed yet hence Cryptocurrency dealing is not restricted.

<u>HELD</u>

The court considered the cases Internet and Mobile Association case and said that as of now there is no specific regulation of Cryptocurrency. The court opined that the 2018 circular has been set aside on basis of unreasonable restrictions that are being set up on the freedom in article 19(i) (g) of the Indian Constitution. Supreme Court reiterated fact and said some institutions are allowing Cryptocurrency as a valid currency for payment. The court also said that Cryptocurrency has the power to create a parallel financial system which shall become a threat to the central regulatory monetary system. RBI has the power to make policies according to the Payments and Settlements Systems Act, 2007.

The transactions related to Cryptocurrency have to comply with the laws like PMLA, NDPS, Tax laws, IPC, FEMA, and RBI regulations related to the KYC and AML regulations. Bitcoin transactions through BINANCE can be managed through Blockchain technology, but it is not following the KYC norms.

The Court ruled that ensuring the legality of the sender and receiver of money, as well as establishing the true identity of the parties and is the obligation of the intermediary which cannot be left to the individuals. It further stated that an intermediate, such as 'BINANCE,' is responsible for ensuring proper measures against activities like 'mixing,' which alters the identification of bitcoins that are run through a bitcoin account, and tracking them is extremely difficult.

[1] V. Ramasubramanian, J., Internet, And Mobile Association of India V Reserve Bank of India, Supreme Court of India, 1, 7, (2020), https://main.sci.gov.in/supremecourt/2018/19230/ 19230_2018_4_1501_21151_Judgement_04-Mar-2020.pdf.

# CHAPTER EIGHT

# GLOBAL APPROACH

Under U.S. regulatory frameworks, a cryptocurrency may be classified as an exchange rate, security, or a commodity (and feasibly more than one at the same time) for U.S. federal law. Whether specific activities using cryptocurrencies are subjected to AML regulatory duties depends on whether the person engaged in those activities fits into one of the "financial institutions" categories defined by the US Bank Secrecy Act (BSA). The Financial Crimes Enforcement Network (FinCEN) (for money services businesses), the Securities and Exchange Commission (SEC) (for issuers, brokers, and intermediaries of securities), and the Commodity Futures Trading Commission (CFTC) (for issuers, brokers, and dealers of commodities) all have their state regulations.

These designations might extend to Anti-Money Laundering regulations to most or all Virtual Currency Exchanges (VCE), several cryptocurrency suppliers, and wallet providers, though the legal framework is still developing. Furthermore, the purview of the state can increase and impose its own licensing and regulatory standards, such as the Bitlicense legislation of the New York Department of Financial Services.

In the United States, the structure for cryptocurrencies AML legislation is most advanced for centralized VCEs. FinCEN issued guidelines in 2013 which concluded that virtual currency is a type of value that substitutes for currency, and that certain people who administer, exchange, or use virtual currencies are considered money services businesses (MSBs) that are subject to the Bank Secrecy Act. FinCEN made a distinction between people who just use "cryptocurrency to purchase goods and services (a user) and those who exchange or administer virtual currency, ruling that the latter two are MSBs until an exemption appears.

In the United Kingdom, officials have taken the position that cryptocurrencies should be considered as a commodity instead of a currency/security. UK Financial Conduct Authority (FCA) chief executive Andrew Bailey has reaffirmed that virtual "commodities" like Bitcoin are unregulated by UK financial regulatory agencies, and any modifications to those laws should be approved by Parliament. 102 Cryptocurrencies like Bitcoin, according to the FCA, are not the "specified investments" according to Financial Services and Markets Act (FSMA)-2000 (Regulated Activities) Order 2001. With the wide range of products that are classified as cryptocurrencies, at the same time there is a risk that some coins or tokens shall be treated as transferable securities which fall under the prospectus regime under the Financial Services and Markets Act 2000 (FSMA) or some ICOs shall be treated as collective investment scheme under section 235 of the FSMA, depending on how they are structured. Derivatives that relate to cryptocurrencies might be regulated investments as well. As of now, Cryptocurrency operations may not fall under the purview of the UK Money Laundering Regulations 2017. Till now 106 Changes are suggested at the EU level which would bring the bitcoin exchanges and custodian wallet providers within the ambit of AML regulations. According to Brexit, the UK will have to incorporate the rules into state legal requirements within 18 months, implying that such changes took effect in 2019.

# CHAPTER NINE

# RECOMMENDATIONS/ SUGGESTIONS

Developing Blockchain technology in Cryptocurrency Money laundering can be prevented. The record should be maintained by the blockchain which makes it an immutable ledger so that it cannot be manipulated; such that it provides security within crypto-asset transactions. A complete record of all the information regarding the transactions should be stored within the blockchain which makes it completely reliable and accurate. So that any illegal activity can be traced back to the source because every transaction can be monitored.

An advanced automated fraud deduction technology can be developed in blockchain such that suspicious transactions can be blocked before implementation. Collaboration with the existing organizations that are operating on blockchain will ensure secure space for Cryptocurrency transactions and can be helpful for crypto businesses and financial institutions to remain safe and free from any risks.

The companies which are involved in Cryptocurrency transactions have o follow the Anti-Money Laundering standards and regulations.

Required changes have to be made to existing laws and regulations like the Prevention of Money Laundering Act-2002, RBI circulars, etc. Provisions should be such that Cryptocurrency business personnel should be included among the persons carrying the designated business/profession and also exchange service provider under the reporting entity section of PMLA Act-2002. An autonomous body should be enacted to monitor the utilization of the currency to provide safety.

A robust code that considers potential complications and risks of trading in cryptocurrencies should be made which helps in regulating and monitoring illegal activities to counteract them.

# CHAPTER TEN

# CONCLUSION

Despite their extreme fluctuation in value and their anonymity, it looks that cryptocurrencies are here to be, at least momentarily being. While seeking to decipher certain complex aspects of India's Cryptocurrency regime, the Court's views, in this case, are a positive step. However, with the rise of cybercrime that knows no territorial or regional boundaries, laws governing virtual currencies (cryptocurrencies) and ensuring the visibility of the money used in cryptocurrency are needed. Regulators/ Authorities in India need to keep up with global advancements in this area and implement suitable steps to successfully control and maintain cryptocurrencies.

Bitcoin at one end provides anonymity because the bitcoin wallets are not linked with KYC, hence it becomes hard to find the source. As it is anonymous it becomes easy to the risks like money laundering. But through blockchain bitcoin is transparent so transactions with date and amount can be found.

Incorporating machine learning technology that allows transactions to be monitored using technology that uses AI technology to effectively sort through strings of meta-data to keep a watch on probable instances of money laundering is one such way that can be implemented. Because A.I.'s pattern recognition capabilities will allow it to detect patterns in massive volumes of data while also adapting to changes in illegal activity over time, this could be a viable option. Even if protective measures are put in place, criminal elements will continue to exist; they will find new ways to achieve their mission, which is to take plus point of the system.

Money laundering is an international problem that no country can handle on its own. Despite the Indian government's attempts to deter such practices, money laundering operations have proliferated throughout the Indian community. The fight over money laundering continues thanks to legislation, administrative organizations, and effective regulators who work ceaselessly in this area. Although such actions may be regulated on a national level, they are not limited to the borders of a jurisdiction. Restraints in one state may encourage money launderers to relocate to another state, which provides a favorable environment for such activities to begin/start.